The Other 95%: Unleashing the Power You Forgot You Had

By Michel Scavuzzo

I0643978

"For my daughter, Emiliana – may you always know the limitless power within you, and never doubt that you are loved beyond measure."

Chapter 1 – Awakening to the Hidden Mind

There comes a moment in life when you realize that the rules you've been living by aren't the rules at all — they're just the story you've been told. Maybe it happens in a quiet kitchen at midnight when you can't sleep and you're staring at your reflection in a dark window. Maybe it's during a walk when your heart feels heavy, and you suddenly wonder if the life you've built is really the one you were meant to live. For some, it happens in the wake of loss or crisis, when the usual scaffolding of life fall...
For me, the moment came when I realized that, despite all my efforts to "think positively" and "work harder," I kept ending up in the same place. I'd set goals, chase them, and sometimes even achieve them, but the satisfaction was fleeting, and the deeper patterns remained unchanged. I was still reacting to life the same way I had ten years earlier. Still feeling the same doubts. Still repeating the same emotional loops.

That's when I discovered the truth: we are not living with one mind, but two — and the one we listen to the most is not the one running the show.

The 5% You Think Is Everything

The conscious mind is the voice you hear narrating your every move. It's where you reason, plan, and make decisions. It's what you use to calculate a tip, remember to pick up milk, or choose a shirt in the morning. We tend to identify completely with this part of ourselves because it's the one we can "hear." But neuroscience tells us that this conscious part is a mere sliver of our mental capacity — roughly 5%.

The other 95%? That's the subconscious — and it's directing far more of your life than you might believe.

Your subconscious isn't just a background process managing your heartbeat and digestion. It's the vast, intricate web of beliefs, memories, emotional associations, and habitual responses that shape how you experience every single moment. It's the silent architect of your reality.

The Hidden Director

Consider this: before you consciously decide whether you like or dislike someone you've just met, your subconscious has already scanned their voice tone, facial expressions, posture, and even micro-smells from pheromones — and made a judgment. By the time your conscious mind forms an opinion, your body and emotions have already decided.

Or think about driving a familiar route. You might arrive at your destination and realize you barely remember the trip. That's the subconscious at work — handling the thousands of micro-decisions needed to get you there while your conscious mind wandered elsewhere.

The real power of the subconscious lies in the fact that it not only acts automatically but also interprets the world for you. Your senses take in far more data than your conscious mind could handle, so the subconscious filters it, delivering only the details it deems relevant based on your past programming.

If you've ever noticed how two people can witness the same event but remember it completely differently, you've seen the subconscious in action.

The Problem With Old Scripts

Here's the catch: most of your subconscious programming wasn't consciously chosen. It was installed in childhood, through repetition, authority figures, cultural norms, and emotional experiences. Between birth and around age seven, your brain is in a highly suggestible state, operating primarily in theta brainwave patterns — the same state hypnotherapists use to access the subconscious.

In those early years, you absorbed everything like a sponge, with no filter to reject what didn't serve you. If you were told "money doesn't grow on trees" or "you're too shy," those statements didn't just bounce off; they became part of your operating system. You carried them into adulthood, where they continued to influence your choices and behavior without you realizing it.

And because the subconscious runs on efficiency, it resists change. It would rather repeat a known pattern — even if it's painful — than venture into the unknown.

My Turning Point

I remember a night when I sat in my small space, surrounded by stacks of self-help books and notebooks full of goals I hadn't achieved. I felt like I'd been running in circles for years. That night, I stopped asking, "What else should I do?" and started asking, "What's really running my life?"

The answer that came — slowly at first, then with blinding clarity — was that I had been trying to create change by speaking only to my conscious mind. I had been like a person trying to steer a massive ship by turning the wheel in the captain's cabin while the autopilot deep in the engine room kept resetting the course.

If I wanted true transformation, I had to go below deck.

Awakening the Other 95%

Awakening to the subconscious is like discovering a hidden room in your house — one that's been there the whole time, quietly influencing everything in the rooms you've been using. At first, it can feel overwhelming to realize how much of your life has been shaped by unconscious patterns. But it's also exhilarating, because once you know the room exists, you can step inside and start rearranging it.

Modern neuroscience and ancient spiritual traditions agree on this point: when you consciously engage with your subconscious mind, you tap into a level of power, creativity, and resilience that feels almost limitless.

From Tibetan monks using visualization to heal the body, to Olympic athletes mentally rehearsing perfect performances, to ordinary people overcoming deep fears in a single breakthrough session — the subconscious is the bridge between what is and what could be.

Your First Exercise

Here's your first step into the other 95%:
Tonight, before you fall asleep, spend five minutes vividly imagining a version of yourself who already lives the life you want. Don't just "think" about it — feel it. Hear the sounds, smell the scents, notice the details. Let the emotions of that reality wash over you as if it were real right now.

Why before sleep? Because in those moments, your brain naturally shifts toward theta waves — the gateway to your subconscious. Feed it an image worth building, and it will start looking for ways to make it real.

The Brain-Body Symphony

The subconscious mind doesn't operate in isolation from your body — it's in constant conversation with it. Your thoughts trigger emotions, which release chemicals into your bloodstream, which in turn influence your thoughts again. This feedback loop is why a single anxious thought can make your palms sweat, and why your body posture can change your mood.

Researchers at the HeartMath Institute have found that the heart sends more signals to the brain than the brain sends to the heart, and these signals can directly influence emotional processing. In other words, by shifting your physiological state, you can send a new message to your subconscious. This is why deep breathing, physical exercise, or simply standing in a confident posture can alter not just your mood, but your decision-making.

Quantum Possibilities

Quantum biology — a field at the intersection of quantum physics and life sciences — offers another layer to this conversation. At the smallest scales, reality doesn't behave like solid, fixed matter. It exists as a field of possibilities, and observation appears to influence outcome. While science is still exploring the practical implications, this aligns intriguingly with what many personal development pioneers have long claimed: that your focus, intention, and emotional state can shape the reality you experience.

When your subconscious beliefs align with your conscious goals, you become a coherent signal in this field of possibilities. People often describe the results as "luck" or "coincidence," but in reality, it's your mind and body working together to select — and create — different outcomes.

Stories That Prove the Point

Take the case of Jim Carrey, who famously wrote himself a check for $10 million "for acting services rendered" long before he became a household name. He visualized it daily, felt the gratitude as if it had already happened, and carried it in his wallet until it became reality. Or consider Dr. Joe Dispenza's patients, some of whom have experienced spontaneous remission from serious illnesses after practicing daily visualization and meditation that reprogrammed their subconscious.

The key element in each of these stories is not just positive thinking, but sustained emotional alignment with a desired reality — a language the subconscious understands.

Your Invitation

As you close this chapter, I invite you to see yourself not as a victim of old programming, but as the author of new scripts. You have an inner operating system that can be rewritten, upgraded, and optimized — and the rest of this book will show you exactly how.

The first step is awareness, and you've just taken it. You've peeked behind the curtain and seen the machinery that drives your life. From here on, you'll have a choice: to keep running the old program, or to step into the other 95% and unleash the power you forgot you had.

Chapter 2 – The Architecture of the Mind

If the subconscious is the hidden powerhouse of your life, then understanding the architecture of the mind is like holding the blueprint to the building you live in. Most people walk through their mental house blindfolded, bumping into furniture, getting lost in rooms they didn't even know existed. But when you can see the floor plan, you understand where you are, how you got there, and — most importantly — where you can go next.

From ancient spiritual maps to modern neuroscience, there is remarkable agreement on one central truth: the mind is not a single, uniform entity. It is a layered, dynamic system with specialized parts, each performing unique roles. The conscious mind, the subconscious mind, and the unconscious mind form the core triad — but each layer has its own hidden substructures.

The Conscious Mind – The Spotlight Operator

Think of the conscious mind as the spotlight on a theater stage. It shines brightly, but only on a small area at a time. It's where we focus, make deliberate choices, and solve problems. This is the mind you're using to read these words right now.

It's a master of logic, but a terrible multitasker. Studies suggest that our conscious awareness can hold only about 7 ±2 bits of information at any given moment — a phone number, a short list, a few thoughts at once. The conscious mind's limitation isn't a flaw; it's a survival feature. By filtering out the overwhelming flood of sensory data, it allows you to function without being paralyzed by too much input.

The conscious mind is also the seat of willpower — but here's the problem: willpower is like a muscle. It can be powerful in bursts, but it fatigues quickly. This is why diets fail, resolutions fade, and new habits crumble if they rely solely on conscious effort. Without the support of the deeper layers, the conscious mind alone is outmatched.

The Subconscious Mind – The Silent Architect

If the conscious mind is the spotlight, the subconscious is the stage, the set, and the backstage crew all rolled into one. It's vast, efficient, and tirelessly at work, managing everything from your muscle memory to your emotional responses.

Here's what makes it so powerful: the subconscious is always on. It doesn't sleep, and it doesn't judge. It simply executes the programs it's been given — whether they serve you or sabotage you.

It stores your long-term memories, learned skills, and deeply held beliefs. It runs your habits automatically, freeing up the conscious mind for other tasks. But its efficiency has a downside: once a pattern is learned, the subconscious resists changing it. This is why breaking a bad habit can feel like trying to rewire a skyscraper while the lights are still on.

The subconscious also speaks a different language than the conscious mind. While the conscious mind thrives on logic and language, the subconscious communicates through imagery, repetition, symbols, and emotions. This is why a vivid, emotionally charged visualization can alter your behavior more effectively than a logical argument.

The Unconscious Mind – The Hidden Archive

Beneath even the subconscious lies the unconscious mind — the deep vault of everything you've ever experienced, whether you remember it or not. It contains repressed memories, unprocessed trauma, instincts, and archetypal patterns inherited from generations past.

Carl Jung referred to part of this as the "collective unconscious," a reservoir of shared human experiences and symbols. Whether you see it as spiritual truth or psychological metaphor, the unconscious holds a raw, primal power. It's the source of our dreams, our shadow self, and the intuitive nudges that seem to come from nowhere.

The unconscious mind can be a source of extraordinary creativity — think of a songwriter waking up with a complete melody in their head — but it can also be the root of irrational fears and self-sabotage. Learning to navigate its depths is a lifelong journey, but even small glimpses can lead to profound transformation.

How the Layers Work Together

These three layers are not separate silos — they are in constant dialogue. Imagine them as three interconnected floors of a building:

- Top floor (Conscious): The control room, making decisions and issuing commands.
- Middle floor (Subconscious): The operations department, running routines based on past instructions.
- Basement (Unconscious): The foundation, holding the archives, instincts, and deep emotional blueprints.

A decision made on the top floor only becomes reality if the middle floor executes it — and the middle floor's work is shaped by whatever is stored in the basement.

If the conscious mind says, "I want to be wealthy," but the subconscious has been programmed with "money is dangerous," the result will be internal conflict and self-sabotage. And if the unconscious holds deep-seated fears of survival, even more subtle resistance can emerge.

Why This Matters for Transformation

Many people fail to change because they focus only on the conscious mind — trying to think their way into a new reality — while ignoring the deeper layers. It's like repainting the walls of a house with a crumbling foundation. The change won't last unless you work from the ground up.

True transformation begins when all three layers are aligned. This requires:

1. Conscious clarity — knowing exactly what you want and why.
2. Subconscious reprogramming — installing new beliefs and habits that support your vision.
3. Unconscious integration — healing and reconciling the deeper patterns that silently influence your choices.

The Neuroscience Connection

Brain imaging studies have revealed that decisions are often made by the subconscious before the conscious mind becomes aware of them — sometimes by several seconds. This suggests that much of what we consider "choice" is actually post-decision rationalization.

Understanding this is liberating, not discouraging. It means that if you can influence the deeper layers, you can change the trajectory of your decisions before they even surface. This is why techniques like hypnosis, guided meditation, and certain forms of therapy can create rapid change — they bypass the conscious mind's defenses and speak directly to the operating system.

Exercise – Mapping Your Mental Blueprint

Take a few minutes to reflect:

- What is one area of your life where you feel stuck or keep repeating patterns?
- Which layer of the mind do you think is driving that pattern? Is it a conscious choice, a subconscious habit, or an unconscious fear?
- Write down one belief you suspect might be shaping that pattern. Is it true? Where did it come from?

Awareness is the first hammer strike in reshaping your mental architecture. In the coming chapters, you'll learn not just to map this blueprint, but to redesign it entirely.

Chapter 3 – Programming the Subconscious

If your subconscious mind is the silent architect of your life, then its programming is the blueprint it follows. This blueprint is not a metaphorical document stored in a drawer — it's a living, breathing network of beliefs, memories, habits, and emotional responses woven into the very structure of your brain and body. And like any blueprint, it can be revised, redrawn, and upgraded.

From the moment you were born — and even before — your subconscious began recording the world around you. Every word spoken in your presence, every tone of voice, every facial expression, every emotional atmosphere you were immersed in... all of it became the raw material for the patterns you live by today. By age seven, much of your core programming was already set.

The Early Coding Years

In early childhood, your brain operates primarily in theta brainwave patterns — the same state hypnotherapists induce to access the subconscious. This means that, as a child, you absorbed information without critical analysis. You didn't filter, question, or challenge the data; you simply stored it as truth.

If you grew up hearing, "You're smart and capable," that became part of your identity code. If you were told, "Money is hard to come by" or "You're not athletic," those too became embedded — not as opinions, but as facts your subconscious works to protect.

This programming also comes through observation. You didn't just hear what your parents said about relationships, success, or safety — you watched how they lived. You saw how they reacted to stress, how they handled money, how they treated themselves and others. These patterns, repeated enough times, became the silent rules your subconscious uses to run your life.

The Repetition Principle

While early childhood is the most impressionable stage, your subconscious can be programmed at any age using the same mechanisms: repetition and emotion. The subconscious learns through consistent exposure. That's why advertisers repeat the same slogans, why coaches drill plays over and over, and why musicians practice scales until they become second nature.

Pair repetition with strong emotion, and the imprint becomes exponentially more powerful. This is why a single traumatic event can override years of calm experiences, and why moments of intense joy or triumph can shift your identity overnight.

The Problem With Accidental Programming

The challenge is that most of your subconscious programming happens accidentally. Media, social environments, cultural norms, and even random comments from strangers can slip past your conscious guard and take root. Over time, these inputs accumulate into an identity script that may not reflect who you truly are — but it feels real because you've rehearsed it for years.

Have you ever tried to set a big goal, only to find yourself sabotaging it without understanding why? That's your subconscious running a conflicting program in the background. It's not trying to hurt you; it's simply executing the code it believes keeps you safe.

Rewriting the Code – The Science

Neuroscience calls this process neuroplasticity — the brain's ability to form new connections and weaken old ones. Every thought you repeat strengthens the neural pathways associated with it. Over time, these pathways become the default routes for your brain's electrical impulses.

This means that when you deliberately focus on new thoughts and feelings, you are literally rewiring your brain. Visualization, affirmations, and emotional rehearsal are not just "feel-good" exercises; they are structural upgrades to your neural network.

Tools for Conscious Programming

1. Visualization with Emotion – Don't just see the goal — feel it as though it's already real. Imagine the sounds, smells, textures, and emotions of success. The more sensory detail, the more your subconscious treats it as a lived experience.
2. Affirmations with Conviction – Repetition alone can feel mechanical, so engage emotion and belief. Instead of saying, "I am confident" in a flat tone, say it while recalling a specific time you felt unstoppable.
3. Environmental Cues – Surround yourself with reminders of your goal — images, music, scents, objects. The subconscious responds strongly to symbolic triggers.
4. Hypnotherapy & Guided Meditation – These can bypass the conscious filter and install new programs directly into the subconscious operating system.
5. Emotional Anchoring – Link a physical gesture or object to a desired emotional state, so you can trigger it on demand.

A Case Study in Transformation

Sarah, a client I once worked with, had a lifelong fear of public speaking. Her conscious mind knew she was capable — she had a PhD and years of expertise — but her subconscious had stored a humiliating childhood memory of freezing during a classroom presentation.

Through a combination of visualization, reframing that old memory, and practicing in safe, supportive environments, she was able to overwrite the fear program. Six months later, she delivered a keynote speech to over 1,000 people — and described it as "the most exhilarating moment of my life."

Exercise – Your Subconscious Audit

- Write down three areas where you feel resistance or recurring problems.
- For each, ask: What belief might be causing this? Where did it come from?
- Decide what new belief you'd like to install, and choose one tool from the list above to begin reprogramming today.

If you understand that the subconscious is not fixed but programmable, you gain the ultimate power: the ability to design yourself. In the next chapter, we'll explore the role of emotions in shaping — and reshaping — your mental blueprint.

Chapter 4 – Emotional Imprints and Memory Loops

Every experience you've ever had leaves a trace in your mind. Some are faint pencil marks, barely noticeable, while others are carved deep like chiseled stone. The deeper the mark, the more likely it is to shape how you think, feel, and act in the future. These deep engravings are what I call emotional imprints — and when they repeat, they create memory loops that can dictate the course of your life without your conscious consent.

An emotional imprint isn't just a memory. It's a state — a combination of sensory impressions, chemical reactions in your body, and meaning assigned by your subconscious. It's the reason a certain smell can bring you to tears, or why a song from high school can transport you instantly back in time.

How Emotional Imprints Are Formed

When you experience something emotionally intense — whether joy, fear, shame, or love — your brain floods with neurochemicals such as dopamine, norepinephrine, or cortisol. This chemical cocktail tells your brain: Pay attention. This matters.

The hippocampus (responsible for memory) and the amygdala (responsible for emotional tagging) work together to store not only the facts of the event but also the emotional tone. This is why you may not remember what you had for lunch last Tuesday, but you can vividly recall the embarrassment of spilling a drink on yourself at a party years ago.

The subconscious treats these imprints as survival data. If an event was linked with danger or pain, it creates a behavioral shortcut to avoid similar situations. If it was linked with pleasure, it encourages repetition.

The Creation of Memory Loops

When a certain imprint is triggered often enough, it forms a memory loop — a pattern that runs automatically whenever you encounter a related situation.

For example, if you were repeatedly scolded for speaking up as a child, the act of raising your hand in class may have been paired with anxiety. As an adult, this loop could cause you to avoid public speaking altogether, even in situations where your conscious mind wants to contribute.

These loops are not inherently bad. They help you brush your teeth without thinking or slam on the brakes when you see a red light. But when they're built from outdated or harmful imprints, they can keep you stuck in patterns that no longer serve you.

The Subconscious Efficiency Trap

The subconscious mind loves efficiency. Once a loop is established, it runs with minimal energy. The problem is, your subconscious doesn't evaluate whether a loop is beneficial — it only checks whether it's consistent with past programming.

This is why a person who consciously wants to be in a loving relationship might continually choose partners who are emotionally unavailable — because the loop of "love equals distance" was imprinted in childhood.

Breaking Free from Old Loops

To break a loop, you have to disrupt its automatic chain of events and replace it with a new one. This involves three steps:

1. Awareness – Recognizing when a loop is running. This often requires paying attention to physical sensations: a knot in your stomach, a tightening in your chest, a sudden rush of heat. These are your subconscious alarm bells.
2. Interruption – Inserting a conscious pause between the trigger and your response. This could be as simple as taking a deep breath, standing up, or even saying to yourself, "Stop."
3. Replacement – Installing a new pattern in the place of the old one. The replacement must be repeated often enough, and with enough emotional weight, that the subconscious adopts it as the default.

Tools for Reprogramming Imprints and Loops

1. Reframing the Original Event – Go back in your mind to the original memory. Imagine watching it from a safe distance, then reinterpret what happened in a way that empowers you.
2. Associative Disruption – Pair the old trigger with a new, neutral, or positive stimulus. If the sound of a particular song triggers sadness, play it while doing something joyful until your brain re-associates the two.
3. Somatic Release – Since imprints live in the body as much as in the mind, use physical practices like shaking, stretching, or breathwork to release stored tension.
4. Anchoring – Create a physical cue (such as pressing your thumb and forefinger together) while in a peak positive state. Later, use the cue when facing a trigger to instantly shift your emotional state.

A Real-World Example

Mark, a successful entrepreneur, could never enjoy his achievements. Every time he hit a milestone, he felt a crushing wave of anxiety instead of pride. Through coaching, he discovered the loop came from childhood, when showing happiness over an accomplishment led to his father criticizing him for "getting cocky."

By reframing the original memory and creating a new celebration ritual with friends, Mark rewired his loop. Now, hitting a milestone triggers joy instead of anxiety — and his business has grown faster than ever because he no longer self-sabotages after wins.

Exercise – Mapping Your Imprints

1. Write down a recurring pattern in your life that you'd like to change.
2. Ask yourself: What memory or feeling comes up when I think about this pattern?
3. Identify the original imprint — the earliest memory of that feeling.
4. Choose one tool from above to begin disrupting the loop.

The beauty of the subconscious is that it can be trained at any age. Emotional imprints and memory loops are not life sentences — they're simply learned programs. And anything learned can be unlearned.

In the next chapter, we'll explore how the body-mind connection plays a direct role in maintaining — or breaking — these loops, and how you can harness your physiology to reprogram your psychology.

Chapter 5 – The Body-Mind Connection

We often talk about the mind and body as if they are separate entities — two distinct systems connected only by the fragile thread of the nervous system. But this is a false division. Your body is not just a vehicle for your mind, nor is your mind merely a command center issuing orders to a passive body. They are one integrated system, constantly exchanging information, shaping each other's state, and working together to create the reality you experience.

This is the body-mind connection — a feedback loop so intricate that modern science is only beginning to understand its full scope. Every thought you think triggers chemical and electrical reactions in your body. Every physical sensation you experience sends signals back to your brain that alter your mood, beliefs, and decisions. This loop is one of the most powerful tools for consciously reprogramming your subconscious — if you know how to use it.

The Bi-Directional Highway

Your brain sends messages to your body through the nervous system, hormones, and neurotransmitters. But it's not a one-way street. Your body sends just as many signals back to your brain through sensory nerves, biochemical messengers, and even the microbiome in your gut.

One of the most striking examples is the vagus nerve — a massive communication highway running from your brainstem through your neck and into your chest and abdomen, touching nearly every organ along the way. Research shows that roughly 80% of the nerve fibers in the vagus nerve carry information from the body to the brain, not the other way around.

This means your physical state can directly shape your mental and emotional state — sometimes more powerfully than conscious thought alone.

How the Body Shapes the Mind

When you adopt a slouched, closed-off posture, you're not just expressing low confidence; you're reinforcing it. Your body position alters your breathing, which changes your oxygen levels, which in turn affects your brain chemistry. Within minutes, your subconscious interprets your posture as a sign of vulnerability, prompting thoughts and feelings to match.

Conversely, standing tall, lifting your chest, and breathing deeply sends a different signal: I am safe, capable, and in control. This is not wishful thinking; it's physiology. Studies by Harvard researcher Amy Cuddy and others show that adopting "power poses" for just two minutes can measurably increase testosterone (linked to confidence) and decrease cortisol (linked to stress).

Your facial expressions work the same way. Even forcing a smile can trigger the release of dopamine and serotonin, lifting your mood — a phenomenon known as the facial feedback hypothesis.

The Gut-Brain Connection

Inside your body, another fascinating system is at play: the gut-brain axis. Your digestive system contains around 100 million neurons — more than in the spinal cord — earning it the nickname "the second brain." The trillions of bacteria living in your gut don't just help digest food; they produce neurotransmitters like serotonin and dopamine that affect mood, focus, and resilience.

This means what you eat can have a direct effect on how you think and feel. A diet high in processed foods can inflame the gut, disrupting these neurotransmitter pathways and leading to anxiety or depression. Conversely, a nutrient-rich diet with plenty of fiber, probiotics, and healthy fats can stabilize mood and sharpen mental clarity.

The Subconscious Loop

The most important takeaway is that your body and subconscious are in constant conversation. Your body reacts to the instructions and beliefs held by your subconscious, while your subconscious updates its programming based on the signals it receives from your body.

If your body is constantly tense, dehydrated, undernourished, or fatigued, your subconscious interprets life as stressful and unsafe — and programs your thoughts and decisions accordingly. But if your body is relaxed, energized, and well-cared-for, your subconscious shifts toward patterns of openness, creativity, and growth.

Using the Body to Reprogram the Mind

1. Breath-work for Nervous System Reset – Slow, deep breathing — especially with extended exhales — activates the parasympathetic nervous system, telling your subconscious that you are safe. This can rapidly dissolve anxiety loops.
2. Movement as Emotional Release – Physical activity doesn't just strengthen muscles; it helps process stored emotions. Practices like yoga, tai chi, or even dance can open the body and release subconscious tension.
3. Posture Training for Confidence – Practice standing and walking as though you've already achieved your goals. This signals your subconscious to align thoughts and behaviors with success.
4. Nutritional Alignment – Eat in a way that supports mental clarity — whole foods, omega-3 fats, probiotic-rich vegetables — to send the subconscious the message: I am cared for and thriving.
5. Sensory Anchors – Use scent, touch, or music to trigger desired states. For example, listening to a particular empowering song every morning can prime your subconscious for confidence all day.

A Real-Life Transformation

James, a client of mine, had battled procrastination for years. Traditional mindset work made little impact — until we addressed his physical state. By changing his morning routine to include breath-work, a short burst of exercise, and nutrient-rich breakfast, his mental clarity and drive soared. His subconscious read his physical vitality as proof that he was ready to take action — and his productivity doubled within a month.

Exercise – The Daily Body-Mind Reset

1. Upon waking, stand tall, stretch your arms overhead, and take three slow, deep breaths.
2. Drink a glass of water to rehydrate.
3. Spend five minutes moving — light stretching, yoga, or a short walk.
4. As you move, visualize your ideal day unfolding successfully.

This routine not only primes your body but also sends your subconscious the message: We are in control. We are safe. We are thriving.

When you master the body-mind connection, you unlock a backdoor to your subconscious. You no longer have to rely solely on mental willpower to create change; you can enlist your entire physical being in the transformation process.

In the next chapter, we'll explore how your subconscious interacts not only with your body but also with the quantum field — and how your thoughts and beliefs may influence reality itself.

Chapter 6 – The Quantum Field and the Subconscious

Imagine the entire universe as an invisible ocean of energy — a field that extends in every direction, connecting every particle, every planet, and every thought. Physicists call this the quantum field, and while the term might sound like something reserved for scientists in lab coats, its implications touch every part of your daily life.

At its core, the quantum field is the fundamental layer of reality. It's not made of matter in the traditional sense — it's made of possibilities. Instead of fixed, solid things, it contains potential states that can manifest depending on how they are observed, interacted with, and influenced.

Your subconscious mind is not separate from this field — it is woven into it. Every thought you think, every emotion you feel, and every belief you hold emits a signal into this field. These signals interact with the web of probabilities and influence which potentials collapse into your physical reality.

Quantum Possibilities and the Observer Effect

One of the most famous principles in quantum physics is the observer effect — the idea that the act of observation changes the outcome. In experiments like the double-slit experiment, particles behave like waves of probability until they are measured. Once observed, they "choose" a location, becoming a particle in a specific place.

While mainstream science debates how far this principle extends into daily life, many researchers and philosophers believe consciousness plays a role in shaping reality. If the universe responds to observation at the smallest scale, then your awareness and focus might also influence which "wave" of possibility becomes your lived experience.

How the Subconscious Sends Signals into the Field

The conscious mind can focus attention deliberately, but the subconscious runs on autopilot — broadcasting signals 24/7 based on your beliefs, emotions, and self-image. If your subconscious is steeped in scarcity, fear, or unworthiness, it will continually project those frequencies into the field, attracting matching conditions and events.

Conversely, when your subconscious is aligned with abundance, gratitude, and possibility, it emits a coherent, empowering signal — one that resonates with opportunities, resources, and connections that match your inner state.

This is not "magic" in the fairy-tale sense. It's resonance. Just as a tuning fork vibrating at a certain frequency will cause another fork tuned to the same note to start vibrating, your inner frequency draws corresponding realities from the field.

The Role of Emotion as an Energetic Carrier

In quantum biology — the emerging field that studies quantum effects in living systems — emotion plays a critical role. Emotion is not just a fleeting feeling; it's a biochemical and electromagnetic state that changes your body's measurable frequency.

Think of your thoughts as the blueprint and your emotions as the electricity that makes the blueprint real. A thought without emotional energy is like a design that never leaves the drawing board. But a thought charged with intense emotion becomes a broadcast to the field, telling it, “This is important. Bring me more of this.”

Coherence: The Secret Ingredient

One of the most powerful ways to interact with the quantum field is through coherence — when your heart, brain, and emotions are in harmony. Studies from the HeartMath Institute show that coherent states produce more stable heart rhythms, balanced brainwave patterns, and clearer mental focus.

When you enter coherence, your body becomes a clear channel for the subconscious to send strong, undistorted signals into the field. This is why meditation, gratitude practices, and visualization can be so effective: they create emotional and mental alignment that the field “reads” as a stable request.

Practical Application: Quantum Visualization

1. Set the Blueprint – Clearly define what you want in specific sensory detail. Picture it in your mind as if it's already real.
2. Charge It with Emotion – Feel the joy, gratitude, or excitement as though it has already happened.
3. Hold the State – Stay in that feeling for several minutes, letting it saturate your body.
4. Release the Grip – Let go of the “how” and “when.” The field responds best when your signal is confident but not desperate.

A Real-Life Example

Elena, an artist struggling to make a living, began a daily practice of quantum visualization. Instead of worrying about sales, she spent ten minutes each morning feeling deep gratitude for her art already being appreciated worldwide. Within three months, she was invited to participate in an international exhibition, and within a year, her work was being sold in galleries overseas.

Skeptics might call it coincidence, but Elena's shift in subconscious programming created a new energetic signal — one that resonated with opportunities she had previously been blind to.

Exercise – Your Quantum Broadcast

1. Write down one goal you want to manifest.
2. Identify the dominant subconscious belief you currently hold about it.
3. Replace that belief with a new, empowering one.
4. Spend five minutes visualizing the goal as already achieved, amplifying the emotional intensity.

The bridge between the subconscious and the quantum field is not superstition — it's a relationship grounded in resonance, coherence, and focused attention. When you understand how to direct your inner state, you begin to realize that your mind is not merely reacting to reality — it is actively creating it.

In the next chapter, we'll explore how to dismantle subconscious resistance so your signals to the field are not sabotaged by hidden doubts or fears.

Chapter 7 – Dismantling Subconscious Resistance

You've probably experienced it before: you set a goal, you commit to change, you even feel motivated — but somehow, progress stalls. You find yourself procrastinating, making excuses, or running into "bad luck" that blocks your path. It's easy to blame willpower, external circumstances, or lack of time, but more often than not, the culprit is something far deeper: subconscious resistance.

Subconscious resistance is the invisible handbrake that slows or stops your movement toward what you consciously want. It's not sabotage in the malicious sense — it's protection. Your subconscious is trying to keep you safe according to old programming, even when that programming is outdated or counterproductive.

Why the Subconscious Resists Change

The subconscious mind's primary job is to ensure your survival. It learns from your past experiences and creates rules to prevent pain or danger in the future. Once these rules are in place, they operate automatically, often without your awareness.

If, as a child, you were laughed at for speaking up in class, your subconscious may have stored the rule: Speaking up equals embarrassment — avoid it. Now, as an adult, even if you consciously want to give a presentation or lead a meeting, that old rule triggers anxiety, procrastination, or avoidance.

The subconscious resists because:

1. It equates the unknown with danger.
2. It sees change as a threat to identity.
3. It prioritizes short-term comfort over long-term growth.

The Three Layers of Resistance

1. Belief-Level Resistance – These are deep-seated ideas about what's possible for you. Examples: "I'm not good with money," "I can't lose weight," "People like me don't succeed."
2. Identity-Level Resistance – The subconscious wants to maintain consistency. If you see yourself as "shy," then acting confidently feels unnatural and will trigger pushback.
3. Safety-Level Resistance – The subconscious will avoid any action it associates with risk, pain, or rejection — even if the conscious mind sees it as beneficial.

How Resistance Shows Up

- Chronic procrastination
- Self-sabotaging habits
- Constant "bad luck" or roadblocks
- Physical symptoms like fatigue or tension before taking action
- Irrational fears that seem to appear from nowhere

Step 1: Identify the Root

The first step in dismantling resistance is awareness. You need to bring the hidden program into the light.
Ask yourself:

- "If I achieved this goal, what bad thing might happen?"

- “When was the first time I felt unsafe trying something like this?”
- “Whose voice do I hear in my head telling me I can’t or shouldn’t?”

Keep in mind, the answer might not be logical — the subconscious deals in emotion, not reason.

Step 2: Create Safety in the Nervous System

Resistance often isn’t just mental — it’s physiological. The body holds the memory of past discomfort. Before pushing forward, signal safety to the body:

- Breathe slowly with long exhales.
- Relax your posture and shoulders.
- Imagine a calming, safe place.

When the body feels safe, the subconscious is more willing to release old patterns.

Step 3: Negotiate, Don’t Fight

You can’t bully your subconscious into compliance — it will only dig in harder. Instead, work with it. Thank it for trying to protect you, and then explain why the change is safe and beneficial. Visualization helps here: imagine your future self-thriving as a result of this change.

Step 4: Rehearse the New Pattern in Low-Stakes Settings

If public speaking terrifies you, don’t start with a stadium crowd. Begin by speaking up in a small, supportive group. If investing money scares you, start with a small amount you’re comfortable losing. This builds trust between your conscious desire and your subconscious safety systems.

Step 5: Anchor Positive Evidence

Every time you take a small step toward the change and it goes well, mark it. Write it down. Feel the emotional satisfaction. This tells the subconscious: See? We did it, and nothing bad happened. Over time, these experiences rewire the old rule.

Real-Life Transformation

Tara, a client of mine, had a lifelong fear of being judged. Her subconscious linked visibility with danger due to childhood ridicule. She wanted to start an online business but found herself procrastinating endlessly. Instead of forcing herself to post publicly right away, we began with small actions: recording videos for herself, then sharing them with a trusted friend, then a small online group. Within six months, she was posting confidently to thousands and enjoying the process.

Exercise – Dismantle a Block in Real Time

1. Identify one area of life where you've been stuck.
2. Write down the fear or "bad outcome" your subconscious is trying to avoid.
3. Take one small, low-risk action toward the goal today.
4. Record what happened and how you felt afterward.

Repeat this process, gradually increasing the level of challenge as your subconscious learns it is safe.

The truth is, subconscious resistance is not your enemy — it's a misinformed friend. Once you understand its motives and retrain its rules, it becomes your greatest ally in creating lasting change.

In the next chapter, we'll explore how to build unstoppable momentum once resistance is cleared, ensuring your subconscious becomes a powerful driver rather than a reluctant passenger.

Chapter 8 – Building Unstoppable Momentum

Momentum is one of the most underrated forces in personal transformation. We often think success is built on discipline, motivation, or sheer willpower, but the truth is, once momentum is established, it takes less energy to keep moving forward than it does to stop. The challenge is that most people never get past the friction of the starting phase — they hesitate, stall, or allow early obstacles to break their rhythm.

In physics, momentum is the product of mass and velocity. The greater the mass and speed, the harder it is to stop. In your personal life, mass is built from consistent habits and supportive structures, while velocity comes from the emotional energy driving your actions. Together, they create a self-sustaining force that propels you toward your goals with increasing ease.

The Physics of Personal Progress

Imagine pushing a heavy car from a dead stop. At first, it requires enormous effort just to get it moving an inch. But once the car is rolling, you don't need as much strength to keep it going — you just have to keep pace. In life, the first push is overcoming resistance, doubt, and fear. Once you've taken consistent action long enough, momentum becomes your ally.

Unfortunately, most people quit before they reach that tipping point. They push for a week or two, see minimal results, and assume it's not working. What they don't realize is that much of their effort in the beginning is spent overcoming inertia, not producing visible results.

Why Momentum Matters for the Subconscious

Your subconscious mind thrives on patterns. When it notices you consistently moving toward a goal without quitting, it upgrades its internal model: This is who we are now. Every repetition strengthens the new identity and makes the behavior feel automatic.

Momentum also works in reverse. If you repeatedly avoid an action, your subconscious assumes it's unsafe or unimportant, reinforcing inaction. The key is to make forward motion the default, so stopping feels stranger than continuing.

The Momentum Formula

1. Start Small, But Start Now – The brain resists big, sudden changes, but it adapts quickly to small, manageable actions.
2. Stack Wins Early – Give yourself quick victories to trigger dopamine, which reinforces the habit loop.
3. Anchor the Habit – Link the new behavior to an existing routine so it becomes part of your daily rhythm.
4. Guard the Streak – Once you've built a chain of consistent action, protect it fiercely. Missing one day is fine; missing two in a row risks collapse.

Emotional Velocity

Momentum isn't just about what you do — it's about how you feel while doing it. If your actions are fueled by dread or resentment, you'll burn out. If they're powered by excitement, curiosity, and meaning, you'll accelerate.

To boost emotional velocity:

- Celebrate micro-wins daily.
- Visualize the bigger picture before each action.
- Surround yourself with people whose energy lifts yours.

Real-Life Transformation

Consider Marcus, a man who wanted to run a marathon but hadn't exercised in years. Instead of forcing himself into grueling workouts, he began with a single minute of jogging a day. Each week, he added another minute. Within six months, he was running 45 minutes without struggle. His subconscious identity shifted from "I'm out of shape" to "I'm a runner." The slow build gave him not just fitness, but unstoppable momentum.

Removing Momentum Killers

Even the strongest momentum can be derailed by:
- Negative Self-Talk – Replace "I can't keep this up" with "This is who I am now."
- Inconsistent Routines – Momentum thrives on rhythm; keep your schedule predictable.
- Toxic Influences – Limit exposure to people or environments that undermine your progress.

Exercise – The 30-Day Momentum Sprint

1. Choose one goal.
2. Define the smallest possible daily action toward it.
3. Commit to doing it for 30 consecutive days, tracking progress visually.
4. At the end, evaluate and scale up.

Momentum turns effort into ease. Once you reach the point where stopping requires more energy than continuing, you've entered a self-sustaining loop — one where your subconscious, body, and environment are all aligned to keep you moving forward.

In the next chapter, we'll explore how to expand your capacity so that once momentum is in place, you can handle bigger opportunities and challenges without losing balance.

Chapter 9 – Expanding Your Capacity

Momentum gets you moving. But if your capacity — your ability to handle energy, responsibility, opportunity, and challenge — remains small, you'll eventually hit a ceiling. That ceiling isn't just external. It's internal, embedded in your nervous system, your habits, and your self-image.

Think of capacity as the size of the container you have for life. If your container is a teacup, even if the universe pours an ocean of abundance toward you, most of it will spill over. Expanding your capacity is about becoming the person who can not only receive more but sustain, manage, and grow what comes.

The Two Kinds of Capacity

1. External Capacity - Skills, systems, resources, and networks that allow you to handle more without burning out.
2. Internal Capacity - Your emotional, mental, and physiological ability to hold larger amounts of pressure, success, and responsibility without collapsing back to old patterns.

Both must expand in harmony. If your opportunities grow faster than your ability to handle them, you'll self-sabotage to return to a comfortable level.

The Nervous System's Role

Your nervous system is like a circuit breaker. When too much energy flows through it — whether that energy comes as stress, attention, money, or responsibility — it trips, shutting you down to protect you from overload.

Signs you've hit a nervous system limit:

- You feel overwhelmed by good news or opportunities.
- You procrastinate on following up with leads or contacts.
- You sabotage wins by making careless mistakes.
- You get sick or exhausted right after a breakthrough.

Expanding capacity requires training your nervous system to feel safe holding more.

Step 1: Gradual Exposure to Growth

Just as you wouldn't lift 200 pounds in the gym your first day, you shouldn't expect to handle massive growth instantly. Increase your "load" incrementally.

- If public speaking terrifies you, start with two people before moving to twenty.
- If managing $1,000 stresses you, learn to budget that before handling $10,000.

Every successful rep tells your subconscious: We can hold more.

Step 2: Strengthen Emotional Regulation

Capacity is directly linked to how quickly you can return to a centered state after being triggered.

- Practice deep breathing to down-regulate stress.
- Use visualization to normalize bigger realities.
- Journal your reactions to challenges so you can see patterns and reframe them.

Step 3: Upgrade Your Self-Image

The subconscious will never allow you to exceed the limits of your identity. If you see yourself as someone who "barely gets by," more money will slip through your fingers. If you see yourself as "socially awkward," bigger social opportunities will feel threatening.

Use affirmations, mental rehearsal, and aligned action to embody the identity of the person who easily holds more.

Step 4: Build Structural Support

The more you can automate, delegate, or systemize, the more mental space you free up for growth.

- Automate recurring tasks.
- Delegate to competent people.
- Create routines that minimize decision fatigue.

Real-Life Transformation

Daniel, a talented chef, dreamed of opening his own restaurant. But when a wealthy investor offered to fund him, he felt paralyzed and almost declined. Through capacity work, he started visualizing himself running a bustling kitchen, practiced managing small catering events, and delegated tasks to his sous-chefs. Six months later, he opened the restaurant and thrived — not because the opportunity changed, but because he did.

Exercise – Capacity Expansion Plan

1. Identify the area where you feel "maxed out."
2. Define the next small step that stretches you without overwhelming you.
3. Schedule consistent practice at that level until it feels normal.
4. Then, move up one level.

Expanding your capacity is not about hustle or adding more to your plate — it's about becoming the version of yourself who can naturally hold and enjoy more without stress. When you do this, momentum doesn't just carry you forward; it carries you upward.

In the next chapter, we'll explore how to align your expanded capacity with your highest vision so your growth is both sustainable and deeply fulfilling.

Chapter 10 – Aligning Capacity with Your Highest Vision

Expanding your capacity is only half the battle. The other half is ensuring that this newfound capacity is directed toward the vision that truly matters to you — not just what's convenient, profitable, or expected by others. Without alignment, you risk building a powerful engine only to drive in the wrong direction.

Your highest vision is not simply a goal. Goals are destinations; a vision is the map, the terrain, and the compass combined. It reflects your deepest values, your most compelling dreams, and the unique contribution you feel called to make in the world.

Why Alignment Matters

Without alignment, growth becomes unsustainable. You might succeed in the eyes of others, yet feel drained, unfulfilled, or even trapped. This is the classic story of the high achiever who reaches the top of the ladder only to realize it was leaning against the wrong wall.

When your vision is clear and your capacity is aligned with it, every step forward feels purposeful. Obstacles become part of the path rather than reasons to quit, and success feels both expansive and energizing.

Step 1: Define Your True North

Ask yourself:

- If I removed all limitations, what life would I design?
- What contribution do I want to make that would still matter 100

years from now?
- What moments in my past made me feel the most alive, proud, or deeply connected?

These answers reveal the themes and values that form the backbone of your vision.

Step 2: Translate Vision into Standards

Your vision must move from the abstract to the tangible. It's not enough to say, "I want to help people." Define how you want to help, who you want to help, and to what extent.

Standards act like guardrails. They ensure that as you expand your capacity, you channel it toward the right opportunities and decline the ones that pull you off course.

Step 3: Audit Current Commitments

You can't align your life with your highest vision if you're already overcommitted to things that dilute your focus.

- List every commitment on your plate.
- Rank them from "fully aligned" to "completely misaligned."
- Begin phasing out or delegating the misaligned ones.

Step 4: Build an Environment That Supports Your Vision

Your surroundings either reinforce or erode your alignment. This includes people, physical spaces, and even digital environments.
- Surround yourself with people who believe in and support your vision.
- Create a workspace that inspires focus and creativity.

- Limit exposure to information or media that distracts or disheartens you.

Step 5: Practice Daily Micro-Alignment

Big visions are lived out in small, daily actions. Every morning, ask: What's one thing I can do today that directly advances my highest vision? This keeps you anchored while still allowing flexibility.

Real-Life Transformation

Ava was a corporate executive earning well into six figures, but she felt perpetually drained. Through clarity work, she realized her highest vision was to use her business skills to help women entrepreneurs in developing countries. Over time, she built her capacity in that direction, gradually reducing corporate commitments and increasing her work in microfinance and mentorship. Today, she runs a thriving nonprofit, and her days are filled with the same strategic challenges she loved — but now, they're fully aligned with her deepest values.

Exercise – Vision Alignment Blueprint

1. Write a vivid description of your ideal life 5–10 years from now.
2. Identify the skills, resources, and relationships you already have that support this vision.
3. Identify the gaps you must fill — and make a plan to fill them.
4. Commit to one aligned action every day for the next 90 days.

When your expanded capacity meets a clear, deeply meaningful vision, you stop chasing fulfillment and start living it. The path ahead becomes not just about what you can achieve, but about the person you're becoming and the legacy you're building.

In the next chapter, we'll explore how to integrate quantum principles into this vision-aligned life, so that your subconscious, your biology, and the universe itself are co-creating your future with precision and power.

Chapter 11 – Quantum Principles in a Vision-Aligned Life

When your capacity has expanded and your life is aligned with your highest vision, the next level of mastery is learning to work with the universe itself. This is where quantum principles enter the picture — not as abstract theories for physicists alone, but as living, breathing realities you can apply to everyday life.

You are not a passive observer of the universe. You are an active participant in a quantum field where energy, intention, and observation interact to shape reality. And when you combine this awareness with a life aligned to your deepest vision, you become a deliberate creator rather than a hopeful dreamer.

The Observer Effect

One of the most profound findings in quantum physics is the observer effect: the act of observation influences the outcome. In life, your focus acts as that observation. When you hold your attention on your vision with clarity and emotional engagement, you subtly shift probabilities in the quantum field toward outcomes aligned with that vision.

Your subconscious mind plays a critical role here. It is the filter that determines which possibilities you even notice, and therefore which ones you can act upon. If your subconscious is aligned with your vision, you become naturally attuned to opportunities, synchronicities, and resources that others overlook.

The Quantum Field as a Canvas

Imagine the quantum field as a vast, vibrating canvas on which infinite possibilities exist simultaneously. Your thoughts, emotions, and actions are the brushstrokes. Every day, you are painting — consciously or unconsciously — a version of reality that will crystallize into your lived experience.

The power lies in intentionality. Most people paint reactively, responding to circumstances. Vision-aligned living means painting proactively, guided by your highest goals and values.

Coherence: Aligning Heart, Mind, and Field

Quantum research and studies in neurocardiology show that the heart's electromagnetic field is more powerful than the brain's. When your heart and mind are in coherence — meaning your thoughts, feelings, and intentions are in sync — your influence on the field becomes exponentially stronger.

Daily coherence practices include:

- Gratitude meditation.
- Heart-focused breathing.
- Visualizing your vision already fulfilled while feeling the associated emotions.

Collapse of the Wave Function

In quantum mechanics, a wave of possibilities collapses into a single reality when measured. In life, this is the moment when potential becomes actual — the opportunity you say yes to, the action you take, the commitment you make.

When aligned with your vision, the decisions you make act as measurements that collapse possibilities in your favor. This is why indecision is so costly; it leaves your energy dispersed among infinite maybes instead of channeled into a concrete yes.

Synchronicity as Quantum Feedback

Carl Jung described synchronicity as meaningful coincidences that seem too perfectly timed to be random. From a quantum perspective, synchronicities may be the universe's way of signaling alignment between your internal state and the external field.

When you notice them:

1. Pause and acknowledge the alignment.
2. Ask, "What's the next step this is pointing me toward?"
3. Act quickly before the energy dissipates.

Real-Life Transformation

Elena, an artist, had struggled for years to sell her work. After doing the deep work of aligning her life with her vision of inspiring social change through art, she began practicing daily coherence and focusing on her highest intentions. Within weeks, she was "coincidentally" introduced to a gallery owner at a café. That introduction led to her first major exhibit, which in turn attracted a nonprofit that commissioned her to create public art installations. What changed? Her frequency — and her conscious interaction with the quantum field.

Exercise – Quantum Vision Activation

1. Spend 5 minutes in heart-focused breathing to enter coherence.
2. Visualize your vision as if it's already real. Feel gratitude and excitement.
3. State one clear intention for today that moves you toward that vision.
4. Take at least one aligned action before the day ends.

When quantum principles are woven into a life of expanded capacity and deep vision alignment, your growth accelerates beyond linear progress. You stop working against the current of life and start surfing the waves of probability, riding them toward the reality you choose to create.

In the next chapter, we'll explore how to dissolve subconscious resistance to these quantum shifts, so your progress remains smooth and unstoppable.

Chapter 12 – Dissolving Subconscious Resistance to Quantum Shifts

You can master quantum principles, expand your capacity, and align with your highest vision — but if your subconscious mind clings to old patterns, you'll experience a frustrating cycle: surges of progress followed by sudden stalls, setbacks, or self-sabotage.

This resistance is rarely conscious. It's embedded in the deep neural and emotional programming your subconscious has built over years, often to protect you from perceived threats. The irony is that the very mechanisms designed to keep you safe can become the chains that hold you back from the life you're now ready to live.

The Nature of Subconscious Resistance
Your subconscious is designed for predictability, not growth. Anything unfamiliar is coded as potentially unsafe, even if it's positive. This is why people sometimes feel anxious after good news or sabotage opportunities that seem "too good to be true."

Resistance can show up as:

- Chronic procrastination.
- Doubting your worthiness.
- Overcomplicating simple steps.
- Starting new things but rarely finishing.
- "Forgetting" to follow through on commitments.

Step 1: Identify the Protective Belief

Every resistance pattern is tied to a core belief like:
- "If I succeed, I'll lose love."
- "I'm not smart enough to handle that."
- "If I'm visible, I'll be judged or attacked."

These beliefs are often installed early in life and reinforced by emotional experiences. The key is to spot the belief without judgment so it can be replaced rather than fought against.

Step 2: Create Safety Around Change

If your subconscious feels safe, it will allow change to happen.

- Visualize yourself thriving in your desired reality while surrounded by supportive people.
- Use small, consistent steps rather than massive, sudden changes.
- Anchor new experiences to positive emotions so the subconscious associates growth with pleasure instead of fear.

Step 3: Rewire Through Repetition and Emotion

The subconscious learns through repetition and emotional intensity.

- Repeat affirmations while in an emotionally elevated state (e.g., after exercise, during gratitude practice).
- Use mental rehearsal to "live" in your desired future repeatedly until it feels normal.
- Celebrate small wins to build emotional proof that change is safe and rewarding.

Step 4: Clear Emotional Blocks

Sometimes resistance is less about belief and more about unprocessed emotional energy stuck in the body.

- Breath-work, somatic therapy, or EFT tapping can help release stored tension.
- Journaling about fears until they lose their intensity can also help free emotional space.

Real-Life Transformation

Marcus had a clear vision of launching a consulting business, but every time he got close, he would "forget" to send proposals or miss follow-up calls. Through coaching, he discovered a deep fear that success would alienate him from his friends, who were struggling financially. By rewriting this belief and visualizing himself succeeding while staying deeply connected to his relationships, he dissolved the resistance. Within three months, his business was thriving.

Exercise – Subconscious Resistance Reset

1. Identify a current goal where you've been stalling.
2. Ask yourself, "What bad thing might happen if I succeed?"
3. Write the answer without censoring it.
4. Create a new, empowering belief that removes the threat.
5. Practice visualizing success while affirming this belief daily for 30 days.

When resistance dissolves, your actions become fluid, your results accelerate, and the quantum shifts you've been cultivating finally lock into place. Instead of moving forward in fits and starts, you progress with steady, unstoppable momentum.

In the next chapter, we'll explore how to create an environment that naturally sustains your quantum growth, so success becomes your new normal.

Chapter 13 – Creating an Environment That Sustains Quantum Growth

Your subconscious mind is shaped by the environment you live in every single day. Even the most disciplined person is influenced — often unconsciously — by their surroundings. If your environment supports your vision, growth becomes almost effortless. If it doesn't, you'll feel like you're pushing uphill, fighting resistance you can't fully explain.

The truth is, your environment is programming you whether you're aware of it or not. The people you interact with, the spaces you inhabit, the information you consume, and even the sensory cues around you are constantly sending signals to your subconscious about who you are and what's possible.

The Law of Environmental Influence

Human beings adapt to their surroundings — it's a survival mechanism. This means you can intentionally curate your environment so that it reinforces the identity, habits, and beliefs of your highest self. Over time, the environment does the heavy lifting, reducing the willpower needed to sustain change.

Step 1: Audit Your Current Environment

Ask yourself:

- Does my home inspire clarity or clutter my mind?
- Do my daily conversations uplift me or drain me?
- Does the media I consume fuel my vision or distract me from it?

Write down every environmental factor that feels misaligned, no matter how small. Even subtle influences, like background noise or wall colors, can affect mood and focus.

Step 2: Upgrade Your Physical Space

Your physical environment should be a mirror of your future, not your past.

- Remove visual clutter. A clear space signals to the subconscious that there's room for new possibilities.
- Place symbols of your vision in plain sight — a vision board, meaningful quotes, or objects that represent your goals.
- Optimize lighting and air quality. Natural light and fresh air boost mood, energy, and creativity.

Step 3: Curate Your Social Environment

You are influenced by the energy, beliefs, and habits of those around you. To sustain quantum growth:

- Spend more time with people who embody the qualities you aspire to.
- Limit exposure to chronic complainers, cynics, or those who belittle your dreams.
- Seek out mentors and peer groups aligned with your vision.

Step 4: Control Your Digital Environment

Your phone and computer are gateways to massive influence over your subconscious.

- Unfollow accounts that trigger comparison or negativity.

- Subscribe to content that expands your thinking and inspires action.
- Set intentional limits on mindless scrolling and news consumption.

Step 5: Align Sensory Cues with Your Vision

The subconscious responds strongly to sensory input.

- Use scents, music, and textures that evoke the emotional state you want to live in.
- Choose clothing that makes you feel confident and aligned with your identity.
- Keep your workspace organized in a way that signals focus and creativity.

Real-Life Transformation

Jared was an aspiring writer who couldn't seem to make progress on his novel. After auditing his environment, he realized he was writing in a dark, cluttered corner of his living room while being constantly interrupted. He moved his desk to a bright window, cleared all distractions, and decorated the space with art and books that inspired him. Within two months, he had written more pages than he had in the previous two years. His environment stopped fighting him and started working for him.

Exercise – Environmental Alignment Plan

1. List three environmental elements that currently hold you back.
2. For each, write one practical change you can make this week.

3. Identify one upgrade you can make to each of these areas:
   - Physical space
   - Social circle
   - Digital space
4. Commit to a 30-day experiment living with these changes.

When you consciously design an environment that supports your vision, quantum growth stops being a struggle and starts feeling inevitable. You're no longer swimming upstream; the current of your surroundings carries you forward.

In the next chapter, we'll explore how to sustain long-term momentum without burnout, so your growth compounds year after year.

Chapter 14 – Sustaining Long-Term Momentum Without Burnout

It's one thing to make a breakthrough — it's another to maintain it for years without losing your spark. Many people hit a surge of growth, only to crash because they've exhausted their physical, mental, and emotional resources. Others stall because they confuse constant activity with true momentum.

Sustaining long-term growth requires a different energy strategy than igniting it. Instead of pouring everything into short-term sprints, you shift into a rhythm that's both powerful and sustainable — like a river that never stops flowing.

The Myth of Endless Hustle

Our culture glorifies hustle — the 16-hour workday, the no-days-off grind — as if it's the only path to success. But hustle without strategy is like trying to sprint a marathon. You burn out, lose focus, and often destroy your health or relationships in the process.

True momentum is about strategic pacing. It's about doing enough to keep moving forward while protecting the very resources — your energy, health, and creativity — that fuel your vision.

Step 1: Adopt Cyclical Energy Management

Nature operates in cycles: day and night, seasons, tides. Your body and mind thrive the same way.
- Schedule deliberate periods of high output followed by intentional recovery.
- Use micro-breaks during the day to reset your nervous system.

- Build in weekly and quarterly rest periods to recharge fully.

Step 2: Define Your Core Activities

Momentum comes from doing the right things consistently, not doing everything. Identify the 20% of activities that generate 80% of your progress and focus relentlessly on those. Delegate, automate, or eliminate the rest.

Step 3: Protect Your Energy Gates

Your energy is finite each day. Guard it fiercely.

- Limit exposure to draining people and environments.
- Say no to commitments that don't align with your vision.
- Create clear boundaries between work and personal time.

Step 4: Anchor in Purpose, Not Pressure

When your actions are fueled by pressure, you run on adrenaline — which is unsustainable. When they're fueled by purpose, you tap into a deeper, steadier energy source. Remind yourself daily why your vision matters, not just what you have to do.

Step 5: Integrate Recovery Rituals

Recovery isn't a luxury; it's a performance strategy.

- Practice deep breathing or meditation to reset your nervous system.
- Move your body daily in ways you enjoy.
- Get consistent, high-quality sleep — the foundation of all sustained performance.

Real-Life Transformation

Tanya built her startup on pure adrenaline, working late nights and skipping weekends. Within a year, her health was deteriorating and her creativity was fading. She switched to a cyclical work pattern, outsourcing non-core tasks and committing to daily recovery practices. Not only did her business grow faster, but she felt more energized than she had in years.

Exercise – Momentum Map

1. Identify your top 3 energy-draining activities and eliminate or delegate them.
2. List your top 3 energy-giving activities and commit to doing them daily.
3. Create a weekly rhythm that includes both high-output periods and scheduled recovery.

When you master the art of sustaining momentum, success stops being a short-lived peak and becomes a lifelong state. You're no longer in danger of burning out or fading away — instead, you move through life like a steady force of nature, unstoppable in your progress.

In the next chapter, we'll explore how to compound growth over decades so the benefits of your quantum alignment multiply far beyond what you can imagine today.

Chapter 15 – Compounding Growth Over Decades

Most people underestimate what they can achieve in 10 years and overestimate what they can achieve in one. The principle of compounding — usually discussed in finance — applies just as powerfully to personal growth, skill mastery, relationships, and impact.

When your growth is aligned, sustained, and built on quantum principles, each year doesn't just add to your life — it multiplies the results of every year before it. Over decades, this creates outcomes so far beyond your starting point that they seem almost miraculous to an outside observer.

The Quantum Nature of Compounding

In quantum physics, tiny changes at the micro level can lead to massive effects over time. Similarly, in personal growth, small but aligned actions — repeated consistently — create exponential results. What seems insignificant in the moment becomes transformative when allowed to build without interruption.

Think of it as planting seeds. A single seed can grow into a tree that produces thousands of new seeds over its lifetime. The earlier and more intentionally you plant, the greater the long-term harvest.

Step 1: Choose Your Compounding Arenas

Not every area of life compounds at the same rate. To create exponential returns, focus on arenas where growth creates more growth:

- Skills – Every skill mastered makes it easier to learn the next.
- Relationships – Long-term trust compounds influence and opportunities.
- Health – Consistent care multiplies energy and resilience.
- Wealth – Financial resources, when wisely invested, generate more freedom to grow in other areas.

Step 2: Optimize for Consistency, Not Intensity

A common mistake is starting with an unsustainable intensity. True compounding thrives on steady, repeatable actions that don't burn you out. A 1% improvement each day leads to massive transformation over years, whereas a 100% push followed by collapse leads to stagnation.

Step 3: Avoid the Erosion Effect

Just as compound growth can work for you, it can work against you if negative habits accumulate over time.
- Poor health choices compound into chronic illness.
- Neglected relationships compound into isolation.
- Missed opportunities compound into regret.

Be as vigilant about avoiding erosion as you are about building growth.

Step 4: Leverage Feedback Loops

Each cycle of growth should feed into the next.
- Review your progress annually.
- Adjust strategies based on results and lessons learned.
- Reinforce what's working and drop what isn't without guilt.

Real-Life Transformation

In her early 30s, Ana committed to learning one new high-value skill each year while maintaining a daily meditation practice and consistent exercise. She wasn't chasing quick wins. Twenty years later, she had become a global leader in her field, built a powerful network, maintained vibrant health, and had the freedom to choose projects that deeply inspired her. To outsiders, her success looked like luck — but it was simply the visible result of decades of quiet compounding.

Exercise - Your 20-Year Growth Vision

1. Imagine yourself 20 years from now, living your highest vision.
2. Identify 3–5 areas where you want exponential growth.
3. Write down one small, daily or weekly action for each.
4. Commit to tracking these actions for the next 90 days as your first compounding cycle.

When you align quantum principles with the patience of compounding, you stop chasing short-term validation and start building a legacy. Over decades, your life becomes proof that greatness is less about sudden leaps and more about consistent, aligned steps — multiplied by time.

In the next chapter, we'll explore how to adapt your vision through life's inevitable changes while keeping your momentum intact.

Chapter 16 – Adapting Your Vision Through Life's Changes

If there's one constant in life, it's change. No matter how carefully you plan your path, life will present unexpected twists — opportunities you never imagined, challenges you didn't foresee, and shifts in your own desires and priorities.

Rigid visions tend to shatter under the pressure of reality. But an adaptable vision — one that can evolve without losing its core essence — becomes unstoppable. Like a river, it can change course while still flowing toward the ocean.

The Power of Flexibility in a Quantum Universe

In a quantum world, possibilities are not fixed. Every decision, interaction, and event alters the potential pathways ahead of you. If your vision is too narrow, you may miss doors that open unexpectedly. But when your vision has flexibility built into its design, you can pivot without losing momentum.

Step 1: Distinguish Between Core and Context

Your core is the essence of your vision — the values, purpose, and ultimate destination that define your life's direction. Your context is the way you pursue it — the specific goals, methods, and timelines.

- Core elements should be unshakable.
- Context should be fluid, ready to shift as conditions change.

Step 2: Practice Scenario Thinking

Instead of clinging to a single future, imagine multiple potential futures. Ask:

- If my current path was blocked tomorrow, what alternative would still honor my core vision?
- How could I achieve my purpose in a different environment, role, or location?

By rehearsing these possibilities mentally, you prepare your subconscious to adapt without panic.

Step 3: Embrace the Growth Reframe

When change feels like a setback, it's easy to slip into resistance. But every shift contains growth potential. The reframe is simple:
- Ask "What is this teaching me?" instead of "Why is this happening to me?"
- Look for ways the change might be clearing a better path forward.

Step 4: Build Adaptation Skills

Adaptability is not just a mindset — it's a skill set. Strengthen it by:
- Regularly learning new skills outside your comfort zone.
- Practicing emotional regulation under stress.
- Staying curious instead of judgmental when facing uncertainty.

Real-Life Transformation

Marcus had a lifelong vision of running a thriving photography business. But when economic shifts and AI tools disrupted the industry, he found his bookings plummeting. Instead of clinging to a failing model, he shifted his focus to teaching photography and selling digital presets online. Within two years, his income surpassed his best photography year — and he discovered a deeper passion for mentoring others.

Exercise – Vision Flexibility Audit

1. Write down your current vision in a single paragraph.
2. Highlight the core values and purposes that must remain unchanged.
3. List 3–5 alternative contexts (methods, industries, locations) where your core vision could still be fulfilled.
4. Identify one area of your life where you could practice adapting now, before it's required.

Adapting your vision doesn't mean giving up on your dreams — it means ensuring your dreams can survive the unpredictable. When you stay true to your core but flexible in your approach, you align with the universe's flow instead of fighting it.

In the next chapter, we'll explore how to build resilience that accelerates growth during times of uncertainty, turning challenges into powerful catalysts.

Chapter 17 – Building Resilience in Times of Uncertainty

Uncertainty is not the enemy — it's the natural state of the quantum world. The very principles that allow for infinite possibilities also mean that life will never be entirely predictable. Resilience is not about avoiding change or shielding yourself from difficulty; it's about becoming the kind of person who can navigate any terrain with clarity, confidence, and purpose.

In the modern world, uncertainty can come in many forms — economic shifts, technological disruption, health challenges, unexpected losses, or global events beyond our control. The difference between those who crumble and those who thrive lies in how well they've built the inner and outer structures of resilience.

The Quantum Model of Resilience

In quantum biology, systems adapt and survive by maintaining dynamic stability — the ability to hold form while adjusting to changing conditions. Similarly, human resilience isn't rigid strength; it's flexibility without breaking.

Think of a skyscraper built to sway during an earthquake. Its flexibility prevents collapse. Your mind, body, and spirit need the same structural adaptability.

Step 1: Strengthen Your Inner Core

Resilience begins within. You must develop an unshakable sense of identity and purpose that isn't dependent on external conditions.
- Know Your Why – A clear, emotionally resonant purpose gives you a reason to keep moving forward when life feels chaotic.
- Daily Grounding Practices – Meditation, journaling, or breathwork stabilize your nervous system, keeping you in a creative rather than reactive state.

Step 2: Build Adaptive Thinking

Rigid thinking cracks under pressure. Resilient thinkers can shift perspectives quickly.
- Reframe problems as puzzles to solve rather than threats to fear.
- Practice solution-focused language: "What can I do?" instead of "Why me?"
- Anticipate multiple outcomes, so you're prepared no matter which way events turn.

Step 3: Maintain Physical Vitality

Your body is your first line of defense against stress.
- Prioritize sleep, hydration, and nutrient-rich food.
- Engage in consistent movement to keep your energy systems strong.
- Use recovery methods — stretching, cold exposure, or massage — to reset your body during high-stress periods.

Step 4: Create Resilient Relationships

Isolation erodes resilience.
- Build a network of people who encourage, support, and challenge

you.
- Invest in relationships before you need them.
- Be willing to both give and receive help — resilience is a collective strength.

Step 5: Embrace Micro-Recovery During Storms

In extended uncertainty, waiting for the “end” to rest is a trap. You must recover in motion.
- Take short breaks daily, even during high-pressure times.
- Use sensory resets — nature walks, music, or even silence — to refresh your mind.

Real-Life Transformation

When the 2008 financial crisis hit, Julia’s business collapsed almost overnight. Instead of withdrawing, she tapped into her resilience rituals — daily meditation, fitness, and calls with mentors. Within six months, she had reinvented her business model and was earning more than before the crash. Her success wasn’t luck — it was the direct result of habits she had built long before she “needed” them.

Exercise – Resilience Blueprint

1. Identify your current biggest source of uncertainty.
2. Write down 3 core practices that would help you stay grounded if that uncertainty intensified.
3. List 2 people you can reach out to for perspective and support.
4. Commit to one daily recovery ritual for the next 30 days.

Resilience is not a personality trait — it's a trainable skill. In the quantum view, uncertainty is not a threat but a field of infinite potential. When you build resilience, you stop fearing the unknown and start using it as raw material for your next breakthrough.

In the next chapter, we'll explore how to accelerate progress by strategically leveraging quantum synchronicities, so opportunities seem to find you.

Chapter 18 – Leveraging Quantum Synchronicities

There are moments in life when opportunities appear as if out of nowhere — you meet the right person at the perfect time, receive an unexpected offer, or stumble across exactly the information you needed. These moments often feel like "luck," but in a quantum reality, they are synchronicities: meaningful coincidences where your inner state aligns with outer events in a way that defies probability.

Most people experience synchronicities occasionally. The difference between those who capitalize on them and those who miss them entirely lies in awareness, alignment, and action. You can't force a synchronicity, but you can create the conditions for them to show up more often and in more impactful ways.

The Quantum Science Behind Synchronicities

In quantum theory, particles can become entangled, meaning the state of one instantly influences the other, no matter the distance. Synchronicity may be a macro-level expression of a similar principle — when your thoughts, emotions, and intentions become energetically entangled with events in the physical world.

In this view, your inner frequency acts like a beacon, drawing in experiences that match your state of being.

Step 1: Clarify Your Signal

Your subconscious mind is constantly broadcasting — through your beliefs, emotions, and focus — what you are "asking" the universe for. If your signal is scattered or contradictory, the synchronicities you attract will be random and inconsistent.

- Keep a short, clear vision statement.
- Visualize it daily, feeling the emotional reality of already living it.
- Remove conflicting beliefs that dilute your signal.

Step 2: Stay in the Field of Possibility

Rigid planning can block synchronicity. While it's important to have direction, you must also leave open space for unexpected opportunities.

- Say "yes" more often to invitations outside your routine.
- Follow intuitive nudges, even when they don't make logical sense immediately.
- Be willing to pivot when a better opportunity appears.

Step 3: Train Your Awareness

Synchronicities often appear in subtle ways — a passing comment, a book recommendation, a sudden thought about someone you haven't seen in years.

- Keep a synchronicity journal.
- Each evening, note any "coincidences" from the day and how they might connect to your intentions.
- Over time, patterns emerge that reveal a larger design.

Step 4: Act Immediately When the Door Opens

A synchronicity without action is a missed opportunity. When the right person, idea, or event shows up, act while the energy is fresh. Delay can dissolve the connection.

Real-Life Transformation

After setting an intention to expand her business internationally, Priya began attending local networking events — even those outside her industry. At one event, she met someone whose cousin owned a company in her target country. Within six months, that single meeting had led to a full overseas partnership. The connection seemed random, but it was the direct result of her clear intention, openness to new environments, and quick follow-up.

Exercise – Synchronicity Activation

1. Write your current top goal in a single sentence.
2. List three feelings you would experience if it were already real.
3. Commit to a daily ritual that keeps you in that emotional state.
4. Keep a 30-day synchronicity log, noting any events, ideas, or connections that align with your goal.

When you live in a way that consistently sends a clear signal, stays open to possibility, notices subtle cues, and acts decisively, you step into a flow where synchronicities become normal. The universe doesn't just respond to you — it collaborates with you.

In the next chapter, we'll explore how to integrate quantum alignment into everyday decision-making so that each choice moves you closer to your highest reality.

Chapter 19 – Integrating Quantum Alignment into Everyday Decisions

Big breakthroughs often come from small decisions. The meals you choose, the conversations you start, the opportunities you accept or decline — each is a quantum choice, rippling out to shape your reality. Most people see these choices as isolated events, but in a quantum framework, every decision is a vote for the reality you will live in next.

Quantum alignment means making decisions that are coherent with your deepest intentions and desired outcomes. It's the practice of bringing your moment-to-moment actions into harmony with your highest vision, so you're not just reacting to life but shaping it deliberately.

Why Everyday Choices Matter

In quantum mechanics, even the smallest particle interactions can produce massive effects over time — the butterfly effect on a universal scale. Likewise, a seemingly minor decision today can initiate a cascade of events that alter the trajectory of your life.

When you operate unconsciously, you give that power away. When you operate with awareness, you start leveraging your decisions as conscious creators do.

Step 1: Identify Your Alignment Markers

An alignment marker is a mental checkpoint you use to measure whether a choice supports your highest vision. Ask yourself:

- Does this action move me closer to my desired reality?
- Does it feel light, expansive, and energizing — or heavy, constricting, and draining?
- Would my future, fully realized self make this same decision?

Step 2: Slow Down the Choice Point

We live in a culture of instant reaction — texts, notifications, and decisions made on autopilot. Quantum alignment requires pausing before acting. Even a 3-second pause can bring your subconscious into the decision-making process, allowing you to act with intention rather than habit.

Step 3: Align Thought, Emotion, and Action

Incoherence — where your thoughts, emotions, and actions are pulling in different directions — dilutes your influence in the quantum field. Coherence amplifies it.

- Thought: Hold the vision of the outcome you want.
- Emotion: Feel gratitude and certainty as if it's already done.
- Action: Take the step that reflects that belief.

Step 4: Leverage Micro-Decisions for Macro Shifts

Major life changes are built on countless micro-decisions. Each healthy meal, each productive hour, each meaningful conversation compounds over time. When even 70% of your daily choices are aligned, you begin to experience exponential growth.

Real-Life Transformation

When Rafael decided he wanted to be financially independent within 10 years, he didn't just focus on big investments — he applied quantum alignment to daily life. He said no to low-value distractions, yes to skill-building opportunities, and chose his circle of influence with precision. Within six years, he had surpassed his financial goals, largely due to hundreds of small, aligned decisions.

Exercise – Decision Alignment Drill

1. Write down your top three life goals.
2. For the next week, track 5–10 of your daily decisions in a journal.
3. For each, note whether it aligned with your goals and how it felt energetically.
4. At week's end, identify patterns and choose one area to improve alignment.

When your everyday choices consistently reflect your highest vision, the quantum field begins to respond in kind. Opportunities that match your energy appear more frequently. Obstacles seem to dissolve. You no longer have to wait for "big breaks" — you create them through continuous, aligned action.

In the next chapter, we'll explore how to maintain your quantum alignment when life throws unexpected challenges your way, ensuring your progress stays intact.

Chapter 20 – Maintaining Quantum Alignment in the Face of Challenges

It's easy to feel aligned when everything is going well — when the opportunities are flowing, the path is clear, and your energy is high. But true mastery isn't measured by how you perform in the sunshine; it's measured by how you navigate the storms.

Challenges — whether financial struggles, relationship breakdowns, health issues, or unexpected losses — test the depth of your alignment. In these moments, your subconscious programming, emotional resilience, and spiritual clarity determine whether you crumble or continue to move forward with purpose.

The Nature of Misalignment Under Stress

Under pressure, the brain often defaults to survival mode — fight, flight, or freeze. This primal response narrows perception, focuses on immediate threats, and can disconnect you from the bigger vision.

In quantum terms, stress can collapse your field of possibilities into a single, fear-based reality. The longer you remain in that state, the harder it becomes to see creative solutions.

Step 1: Pause Before Reacting

When crisis strikes, your first task is to create energetic space between the event and your response.
- Breathe deeply and slowly to shift your nervous system out of survival mode.
- Delay major decisions until emotional intensity has settled.
- Remember: responding from fear creates more fear-based outcomes.

Step 2: Reconnect to Your Core Vision

Your vision acts as a north star during uncertainty.
- Read or recite your vision statement daily, especially during challenging periods.
- Visualize the desired outcome as if the challenge has already been resolved.
- Anchor into the emotional frequency of your end goal, not the current obstacle.

Step 3: Adjust Without Abandoning

Alignment is not rigidity. Sometimes the path must shift while the destination stays the same.
- Ask, "What is the highest-aligned action I can take right now?"
- Be open to alternative routes that still lead to your intended outcome.
- Remember: the obstacle may be the catalyst that brings you to a better path.

Step 4: Surround Yourself With Stabilizers

The people and environments you immerse yourself in will either amplify your fear or your faith.

- Lean on mentors, friends, or communities that share your vision and values.
- Limit exposure to news, gossip, and negative energy that drags you off alignment.
- Seek environments — even if temporary — that restore your calm and clarity.

Step 5: Extract the Gift From the Challenge

Every challenge contains a quantum seed of opportunity — a lesson, a connection, or a shift in perspective that could not have emerged otherwise.

- Journal daily on the question: "What is this teaching me?"
- Identify skills or strengths the challenge is helping you develop.
- Look for the unexpected doors that open during the process.

Real-Life Transformation

When Malik's business partner unexpectedly left — taking key clients with him — it felt like everything he'd built was crumbling. Instead of reacting impulsively, Malik spent the first week in reflection, focusing on his vision rather than revenge or panic. That space allowed him to rebrand, develop new services, and attract clients more aligned with his long-term goals. Within a year, his revenue exceeded what it had been before the split.

Exercise – Alignment Under Pressure

1. Identify a current or past challenge that shook your sense of alignment.
2. Write down three ways you could have (or did) pause before reacting.
3. List the core elements of your vision that remained unchanged despite the challenge.
4. Identify one "gift" or opportunity that emerged from the experience.

Maintaining alignment in the face of challenges is about staying anchored in your highest reality, even when the waters around you are turbulent. The more you practice this skill, the less external events have power over your internal state — and the faster you recover when life tests you.

In the next chapter, we'll explore how to expand your influence in the quantum field so your vision impacts not only your life but the lives of others around you.

Chapter 21 – Expanding Your Influence in the Quantum Field

Your personal quantum field is not an isolated bubble; it's a living, dynamic network that interacts with the fields of every person, place, and possibility you encounter. The frequency you emit doesn't just shape your life — it subtly influences the lives of others. This is how a single inspired person can spark movements, shift cultures, and alter the course of history.

The greater your coherence — the alignment between your thoughts, emotions, and actions — the stronger your broadcast signal. And just like a radio tower, the more powerful and clear your signal, the further it travels and the more lives it touches.

The Ripple Effect of Coherence

In physics, coherent waves amplify one another, creating stronger and more stable patterns. In human interaction, coherence works the same way. When your presence is grounded, purposeful, and infused with positive intention, you "phase-lock" with others, uplifting their state without saying a word.

Step 1: Strengthen Your Signal

- Daily Alignment Practice: Start each day aligning your mind, emotions, and body with your desired reality. Meditation, visualization, and breathwork are powerful tools.
- Energetic Hygiene: Limit exposure to toxic environments and people who consistently pull your energy into incoherence.
- Embodiment: Live your values visibly — let your actions demonstrate your alignment.

Step 2: Influence Through Presence, Not Pressure

People are more receptive to energy than to words. Rather than forcing your perspective, model the state of being you wish to inspire. This silent broadcast often shifts others more deeply than persuasion.

Step 3: Create Resonance Points

Identify the environments where your frequency naturally amplifies:

- Creative spaces where ideas flow.
- Communities aligned with your vision.
- Projects that make you lose track of time.

The more time you spend in these high-resonance spaces, the more your influence grows.

Step 4: Contribute Without Expectation

Contribution without strings attached creates trust and magnetic reciprocity. When you add genuine value to others 'lives, the quantum field often returns that value in unexpected and amplified forms.

Real-Life Transformation

Elena, a small-town yoga instructor, began posting short, heartfelt meditations online without the goal of growing her business. Her calm, coherent presence resonated with thousands, then millions. Within two years, she was invited to lead global retreats and partner with wellness leaders worldwide — all because her broadcast frequency was consistent, authentic, and generous.

Exercise – Quantum Influence Mapping

1. List five people whose lives you could positively impact within the next 30 days.
2. Identify the qualities you want to embody for them — clarity, encouragement, empowerment, etc.
3. Take one aligned action toward each person without expecting anything in return.
4. Track any unexpected opportunities or connections that arise as a result.

Your influence in the quantum field grows not by chasing power, but by deepening your coherence and living your highest alignment openly. As your signal strengthens, it naturally synchronizes with others who are ready for transformation, creating ripples that can extend far beyond your personal reach.

In the next chapter, we'll explore how to sustain this expanded influence without burning out, ensuring your energy remains abundant and your impact continues to grow.

Chapter 22 – Sustaining Expanded Influence Without Burnout

Influence in the quantum field can feel exhilarating — opportunities multiply, people seek your guidance, and your work begins creating ripples far beyond what you can see. But if you're not careful, that expansion can also become overwhelming. The same energy that fuels your impact can drain you if it's not managed intentionally.

Burnout is not simply the result of "doing too much"; it's a sign that you've been giving from depletion rather than overflow. In quantum terms, it's a signal that your energetic field has been outflowing without enough inflow to sustain it.

Step 1: Anchor Into Your Energy Baseline

Before you can manage your influence sustainably, you must know your energetic baseline — the state in which you feel balanced, focused, and replenished.

- Identify the daily habits that keep you in this state (sleep, meditation, creative time, nature, etc.).
- Treat them as non-negotiable, not luxuries.
- Monitor for subtle signs of depletion before they become full burnout.

Step 2: Practice Conscious Output

Not every request, opportunity, or collaboration deserves your "yes." Expansion without discernment is a direct path to exhaustion.

- Ask: "Does this opportunity amplify my core vision or scatter my focus?"
- Evaluate whether the energetic cost is worth the potential outcome.
- Give yourself permission to say no without guilt — a strong signal of self-respect in the quantum field.

Step 3: Maintain Energy Reciprocity

When influence grows, more people will want to receive from you — advice, time, energy, resources. To avoid depletion:

- Build relationships where energy flows both ways.
- Invest more deeply in connections that nourish you as much as you nourish them.
- Limit prolonged exposure to those who only take without giving.

Step 4: Create Structured Renewal

Energy renewal must be scheduled with the same priority as key projects.

- Plan regular retreats, even if just a weekend at home without obligations.
- Engage in activities that restore your flow state — art, music, movement, travel, spiritual practice.
- Set boundaries around availability, especially in digital communication.

Step 5: Trust the Quantum Field to Carry the Message

Many burn out because they feel they must personally "hold it all together." But in quantum reality, your influence is not limited to your direct actions. Once you've set something in motion with clarity and intention, the field continues working with it — even when you step back to rest.

Real-Life Transformation

When Aisha's coaching practice exploded in popularity, she doubled her client load to meet demand. Within months, she was exhausted and considering quitting altogether. By restructuring her offerings into group programs, setting firm boundaries on her availability, and scheduling regular personal retreats, she maintained her influence while working fewer hours — and her income and impact both grew.

Exercise – Influence Sustainability Plan

1. Define your ideal energetic baseline and list three habits that maintain it.
2. Identify two current commitments you can decline or delegate to preserve energy.
3. Plan one renewal activity for the next 7 days and treat it as non-negotiable.
4. Reflect on one area where you can trust the quantum field to carry the work without constant intervention.

Sustaining influence without burnout is not about doing less — it's about doing what matters most, from a place of energetic abundance. The more you operate from overflow, the stronger and longer-lasting your impact becomes.

In the next chapter, we'll explore how to leave a lasting quantum legacy — ensuring your influence endures and expands even beyond your lifetime.

Chapter 23 – Leaving a Lasting Quantum Legacy

Most people think of legacy as something material — money, property, or a name remembered in history books. But in quantum reality, your true legacy is energetic. It's the frequency you leave imprinted on the collective field, the ripple your existence sends out long after your physical presence is gone.

This legacy is not built in grand, singular moments — it's crafted daily, through the thoughts you hold, the emotions you embody, the actions you take, and the influence you radiate.

Step 1: Define Your Legacy Intentionally

Many live without consciously shaping the mark they leave on the world. In the absence of intention, your legacy becomes accidental — shaped by unconscious patterns, reactive choices, and societal conditioning.

- Ask yourself: "What do I want people to feel because I lived?"
- Identify the core values you want to leave behind — compassion, courage, curiosity, empowerment, love, truth.
- Align your daily life with those values so your legacy is built in real time.

Step 2: Build Legacy Through Relationships

While achievements may fade, the energy you leave in others 'hearts often lasts generations.

- Mentor someone who can carry your wisdom forward.
- Treat each interaction as a chance to leave someone better than you found them.
- Invest in deep, authentic connections rather than surface-level networking.

Step 3: Create Quantum Artifacts

Your words, creations, and contributions to the world carry your frequency into the future.

- Write books, record messages, create art, develop ideas that encapsulate your values.
- Leave behind physical or digital creations that can inspire people long after you're gone.
- Ensure these artifacts reflect your highest truth, not just your current circumstances.

Step 4: Plant Seeds You'll Never See Grow

True legacy often involves contributing to something bigger than yourself, without the guarantee of seeing the outcome.

- Support causes or movements aligned with your vision.
- Contribute knowledge or resources anonymously, purely for the sake of impact.
- Think generationally — what will still matter 50, 100, or 500 years from now?

Step 5: Live Your Legacy Now

Your legacy is not a future event — it's being built every time you choose alignment over fear, generosity over scarcity, truth over convenience. In quantum terms, each aligned action strengthens your field's imprint in the collective, making your influence more enduring.

Real-Life Transformation

When Samuel, a community leader, passed away unexpectedly, his town discovered countless acts of kindness he'd done in secret — paying off grocery bills, mentoring troubled teens, anonymously funding local projects. His influence continued long after his death because the energy of his service was woven into the lives of hundreds of people, who then carried that energy forward in their own actions.

Exercise – Quantum Legacy Blueprint

1. Define in one sentence the energetic impact you want to leave on the world.
2. List three values that will form the foundation of your legacy.
3. Identify one person you can mentor or influence positively this month.
4. Begin one "quantum artifact" — a piece of work or message that will carry your essence into the future.

Leaving a quantum legacy is not about being remembered — it's about ensuring that the frequency you lived by continues to inspire, empower, and uplift long after you're gone. Every aligned thought, word, and action you take today is a brushstroke on the masterpiece of your lasting impact.

In the next chapter, we'll explore how to ensure your quantum evolution continues even beyond this lifetime, stepping into the concept of consciousness as an ongoing journey.

Chapter 24 – Continuing Quantum Evolution Beyond This Lifetime

If consciousness is not confined to the body — if it is truly a field of awareness that transcends physical form — then death is not an ending but a transition. In the quantum view, your personal frequency doesn't vanish; it disperses, integrates, and continues evolving in the greater field of intelligence that underlies all existence.

The idea that your growth, your influence, and your awareness could continue beyond this lifetime is not just a spiritual comfort; it is a principle rooted in the nature of energy itself. Energy is never destroyed, only transformed — and consciousness, being a form of subtle energy, follows the same law.

Step 1: Understanding the Continuity of Consciousness

Throughout history, cultures across the globe have taught that the soul or spirit exists beyond the body. From Tibetan Buddhism's teachings on the bardo states to Indigenous understandings of ancestral presence, the belief in continuity has deep, cross-cultural roots. Quantum biology adds a fascinating layer — if our thoughts and intentions are patterns of information in the quantum field, those patterns may persist even when the biological vessel changes form.

Step 2: Expanding Awareness While You're Here

Your preparation for post-physical evolution begins now. The more coherent, expanded, and loving your consciousness is in life, the more fluidly it may integrate into higher states after death.

- Self-awareness practices like meditation and lucid dreaming help you explore non-physical states now.
- Emotional mastery allows you to navigate challenging energetic environments beyond the body.
- Purpose alignment ensures your energy signature is strong and stable.

Step 3: Building Bridges Through Legacy Frequencies

Everything you've created in this lifetime — relationships, art, acts of service — is encoded with your frequency. These "legacy frequencies" act as bridges between your current self and the quantum field after you transition. They carry your essence forward and keep the pathway open for continued influence and interaction.

Step 4: The Role of Quantum Imprinting

Think of your life as a constant process of imprinting the quantum field with your unique signal. Each choice, intention, and creation strengthens that imprint. Over decades, you can weave a rich, resonant signal into the field — one that not only persists after your death but continues to interact with and inspire the living.

Step 5: Conscious Transition Practices

Traditions such as Tibetan phowa (conscious dying) or yogic mahasamadhi are based on entering death with clarity and intention. While you may or may not adopt these exact practices, you can:

- Regularly reflect on your impermanence without fear.
- Maintain emotional closure in relationships as much as possible.
- Create a personal "transition vision" — how you intend to meet that threshold with openness and grace.

Real-Life Transformation

Elena, a hospice volunteer, practiced deep meditation daily and intentionally infused her interactions with unconditional love. In her final weeks, she described visions of vast light fields and familiar energies awaiting her. After her passing, multiple friends reported vivid dreams of her offering encouragement — a striking reminder that connection may extend beyond the veil.

Exercise – Preparing for Continued Evolution

1. Write a one-page "transition manifesto" — a declaration of how you wish to leave this life energetically.
2. Identify three habits that expand your awareness and commit to deepening them.
3. Begin one creation (art, writing, recording, teaching) that will carry your essence forward.
4. Release one lingering emotional burden or unresolved conflict.

Death is not the end of your quantum evolution; it is simply a gateway into another form of being. By living in alignment now, you not only create a rich, meaningful life — you also set the trajectory for whatever lies beyond, ensuring your frequency continues to explore, contribute, and expand in the infinite field.

In the final chapter, we'll explore how to integrate all 25 chapters into a unified life practice, so this isn't just a book you've read, but a transformation you live.

Chapter 25 – Integrating the Other 95% Into a Unified Life Practice

You've journeyed through twenty-four chapters exploring the hidden depths of your subconscious mind, the profound intelligence of your quantum biology, and the vast interplay between your personal frequency and the universe around you. Along the way, you've unlocked principles, methods, and perspectives that, if lived rather than simply understood, can rewrite the story of your life.

But knowledge alone does not create transformation — integration does. The true alchemy happens not in reading, but in living what you've learned until it becomes second nature. The final step is weaving these insights into a unified practice — not as a checklist, but as a way of being.

Step 1: Design Your Daily Quantum Ritual

Your subconscious is shaped most powerfully by repetition. Consistent daily habits are the scaffolding that hold the architecture of your transformation.

- Morning Alignment – Begin each day by setting your frequency: visualize your desired reality, breathe into gratitude, and affirm your highest identity.
- Midday Calibration – Pause to check your emotional state and re-align if necessary.
- Evening Integration – Reflect on the day, acknowledge where you lived in alignment, and release anything that doesn't serve tomorrow's vision.

Step 2: Live From the Identity of Your Future Self

Every decision is an opportunity to choose who you are becoming. Let your envisioned self be the compass that guides action. Ask before choices big and small:
"Is this what my highest self would choose?"

By repeatedly choosing from that place, you collapse the time between who you are and who you want to be.

Step 3: Balance Expansion with Restoration

You've learned that influence in the quantum field thrives when you are in overflow, not depletion. Integrating rest, joy, and play into your life is not laziness — it's quantum maintenance. Protecting your energy keeps your frequency pure and powerful.

Step 4: Keep Curiosity Alive

While this book closes here, your journey is just beginning. Curiosity is the doorway to continued quantum growth. Ask new questions daily. Explore beyond your comfort zones. The moment you think you've "arrived" is the moment your evolution slows.

Step 5: Share and Amplify the Ripple

The quantum field responds to contribution. By teaching, mentoring, and sharing what you've learned, you not only reinforce your mastery but also multiply your influence. The more you give from abundance, the more the field reflects abundance back to you.

A Final Story — The Endless Horizon

In coastal towns around the world, there are places where you can stand on a cliff and watch the ocean fade into the horizon. No matter how far you sail, the horizon never ends — it simply reveals more. This is the nature of quantum reality. Your growth, your influence, and your capacity to create are not finite; they are an endless horizon waiting for you to keep going.

Your Ongoing Journey With Me

This book has been your introduction to The Other 95% — a framework for awakening the dormant power you've always had. But this is only the beginning. In the months and years ahead, I'll be releasing more works that dive deeper into specific aspects of this path:

- Advanced subconscious reprogramming techniques
- Expanded quantum biology applications
- Collective consciousness influence
- Practical spirituality for a modern world

These books will be designed not only to educate, but to activate you at an even higher level.

You now hold the keys to a reality most people never imagine possible. The question is not whether the quantum field will respond — it already is. The question is, will you keep showing up as the person who can receive everything you've been asking for?

The Other 95% is yours now. Live it. Breathe it. Become it. And when you're ready for the next horizon, there will be more chapters to come that are yet to be written...

www.ingramcontent.com/pod-product-compliance
Lightning Source LLC
LaVergne TN
LVHW020320061026
849616LV00032B/468
* 9 7 9 8 2 1 8 7 6 6 5 1 1 *